BOOK OF
ROCK 'N' ROLL

THE LITTLE BLACK LEATHER

BOOK OF

ROCK 'N' ROLL

Compiled

& Annotated by

DIVINE LABORATORIES

A LITTLE RED BOOK

ARSENAL PULP PRESS

A little red book

THE LITTLE BLACK LEATHER BOOK
OF ROCK 'N' ROLL
COPYRIGHT © 1994
BY DIVINE LABORATORIES
All rights reserved.
ISBN 1-55152-003-6
CIP DATA: *see page 6*

LITTLE RED BOOKS
are published by
ARSENAL PULP PRESS
1062 HOMER STREET #100
VANCOUVER BC V6B 2W9

COVER ILLUSTRATION:
Eve Corbel
TYPESETTING: *Vancouver Desktop*
PRINTING: *Webcom*
PRINTED AND BOUND IN CANADA

TABLE OF CONTENTS

CATALOGUING IN PUBLICATION DATA

Main entry under title:
The Little black leather book of rock 'n'
roll
(A Little red book)
ISBN 1-55152-003-6
1. Rock music—Quotations, maxims, etc.
2. Quotations, English.   I. Divine
Laboratories (Association).   II. Series.
ML3534.L57 1994   781.66'09
C94-910398-5

INTRODUCTION

Rock 'n' roll is unquestionably the dominant musical form of the late twentieth century—and more than that, may be the epoch's dominant form of expression of any kind. Rock 'n' roll is pervasive the world over, agent and voice of both the corporate culture and the counter-culture. It is a hybrid of attitudes and language, of youth and style, and at times seems to propose a very way of being in the world.

So how did it come to pass? Where did it come from? Where is it going? How has rock 'n' roll become so *huge*? Or perhaps there are larger, more relevant questions to ask, questions which will get to the heart of what rock 'n' roll is *really* about. Such as:
—Is rock 'n' roll the devil's music?

—Has Elvis gone back to truck driving?
—Does one require a penis to play the electric guitar?
—Will rock 'n' roll make one rich, beautiful, and successful?
—Does rock 'n' roll lead to harder stuff?
—Does hairspray on the lens really make one sound better?
—Is reading about rock 'n' roll like swimming about architecture?

We can only hope this gathering of remarks from the Great and the near-Great in the world of rock 'n' roll will help to illuminate the quintessential mystery of the age.

Let's face it, rock 'n' roll is bigger than all of us. —ALAN FREED

THE QUOTATIONS

Rock 'n' roll does for music what a motorcycle club at full throttle does for a quiet afternoon. The results bear passing resemblance to Hitler mass meetings.
— *Time (1956)*

Rock music is a necessary step in the evolution of man, as was LSD, Hitler, the electric light and everything else.
— *Mel Lyman*

Rock 'n' roll is a communicable disease.
— *New York Times (1956)*

Rock 'n' roll was getting up there, stepping out and creating the greatest possible imperfection.   — *Malcolm McLaren*

Rock 'n' roll is so great that everyone in the world should think it's the greatest thing that's happening. If they don't, they're turds.   — *Lux Interior, The Cramps*

If it makes you move, or moves you, or grooves you, it'll be here. The blues rolls on, rock steady knocks, and they all are here now and I think they all will be here from now on.

— *Chuck Berry*

That's what it's all about—filling up the chest cavities and the empty kneecaps and elbows.

— *Jimi Hendrix*

Rock 'n' roll starts between the legs and goes through the heart, then to the head. As long as it does those three things, it's a great rock song.

— *John Mellencamp*

Rock 'n' roll is part of a pest to undermine the morals of the youth of our nation. It is sexualistic, unmoralistic and . . . brings

people of both races together.
— *North Alabama White Citizens' Council
(1950s)*

Poison put to sound. — *Pablo Casals*

Rock 'n' roll is an asylum for emotional imbeciles. — *Richard Neville*

At what point did rhythm and blues start becoming rock 'n' roll? When the white kids started to dance to it.
— *Ruth Brown*

It has no beginning and no end, for it is the very pulse of life itself.
— *Larry Williams*

At a party with friends, have a ball!—ROCK!—to the rock side OR listen to the dreamy side with your "special person". It

will bring you closer together.
> — *D.J. Art Laboe*, liner notes, Oldies But
> Goodies, Vol III *(1966)*

It's not music, it's a disease.
> — *Mitch Miller*

It's primarily not an intellectual thing.
> — *Jann Wenner, editor*, Rolling Stone

I made a mistake thinking that rock 'n' roll had something to do with being intelligent and not accepting society as it was being given to us.
> — *Ian MacKaye, Fugazi*

Rock 'n' roll actually wasn't invented by anybody, and it's not just black and white either. It's Mexican and Appalachian and Gaelic and everything that's come floating down the river.
> — *T-Bone Burnett*

There's something unnatural about white

artists doing it to me.

— *Phil Spector*

There might be a possibility that rock 'n' roll is primal therapy. If you have to yell at 100dB, you have to take out some of your stuff. — *Grace Slick*

Rock 'n' roll is quite fun and everything, but I'm only using it as a medium.

— *David Bowie*

Basically, rock & roll is all about looking good, living fast and dying young.

— *Joe Jackson*

Rock 'n' roll all goes back to R&B, but to me it's not very relevant. Kraftwerk is much more relevant.

— *Nick Rhodes, Duran Duran*

Rock 'n' roll is beautiful and it's ugly simultaneously. I mean, it's rock 'n' roll that brings people together in the mud in Woodstock. It's rock 'n' roll that starts black riots in Rochester and has cops beating people on the head for ten hours later. It's rock 'n' roll, you know, there's so many good things, and so many bad things. It's so unpredictable.   — *Howard Stein*

Rock 'n' roll is like an aphrodisiac for people who have everyday jobs and shit.
     — *Slash, Guns N Roses*

Rock 'n' roll is the lowest form of life known to man.   — *Elvis Costello*

I'm into revolution and radicalism and changing the whole world structure.
     — *Kathleen Hanna, Bikini Kill*

I am interested in anything about revolt, disorder, chaos, especially activity that seems to have no meaning.
     — *Jim Morrison*

Not even boot camp is as tough as being in rock 'n' roll. — *Patti Smith*

Rock 'n' roll was two pegs below a prisoner of war back then.

— *Ronnie Hawkins*

I don't know if prison is good for everybody, but it did me a lot of good.

— *Hugh Cornwell, The Stranglers*

It's not like being in band is all that fun or anything. — *J. Mascis, Dinosaur Jr.*

I bit the head off a live bat the other night. It was like eating a Crunchie wrapped in chamois leather. — *Ozzy Osbourne*

I don't bite the heads off chickens or frighten horses, but I've survived in this business for years. I like gardening and growing vegetables at home.

— *Tony Banks, Genesis*

Nobody gives Colonel Sanders the stick I've had and he murders about nine million chickens a day.   — *Ozzy Osbourne*

Middle-class kids make the best rock 'n' roll.   — *Elliott Murphy*

Rhythm is something you either have or don't have, but when you have it, you have it all over.   — *Elvis Presley*

There's a basic stupidity in the music industry, the bands, the awards. The whole thing is on an intelligence level that's really substandard.

          — *Exene Cervenka, X*

Not only are most rock 'n' roll songs junk, but in many cases, obscene junk pretty much on a level with dirty comic magazines.   — *Billy Rose*

It's really exciting! It's great! I'm really

knocked out! It's wonderful!

— *Kate Bush*

The whole scene makes me a bit sick.

— *Bonnie Raitt*

Rock music is the most brutal, ugly, vicious form of expression—sly, lewd, dirty—a rancid-smelling aphrodisiac—martial music of every delinquent on the face of the earth.   — *Frank Sinatra*

I wanted to be a singer because I didn't want to sweat.   — *Elvis Presley*

Gosh, he's so great. You have no idea how great he is, really you don't. You have no comprehension—it's absolutely impossible. I can't tell you why he's so great, but he is. He's sensational. . . . The unquestionable king of rock 'n' roll.

— *Phil Spector*

Laugh but that's what they called me, and that's what some still call me: The King of Rock 'n' Roll.

— *Carl Perkins*

There have been a lotta tough guys. There have been pretenders. There have been contenders. But there is only one king.

— *Bruce Springsteen*

Somebody has to be the boss.

— *Elvis Costello*

Elvis had animal magnetism. He was even sexy to guys. I can't imagine what the chicks used to think.

— *Ian Hunter*

We used to love Elvis 'til we saw Depeche Mode.   — *David Carswell, The Smugglers*

I don't know anything about music—in

my line you don't have to.

— Elvis Presley

There's a man in West Memphis, has a recording studio there. He recorded me once . . . but he ain't never gonna do it again. He gave my song to someone else, and put it out on record, and says that he'd written it. So he got money for the song. That motherfucker! I went there to his house in West Memphis and hid in the grass outside his house with a pistol. But when I was gonna shoot him, his wife came home. I was mad. I would have shot him.

— John "Red" Williams

He took my music. But he gave me my name.   *— Muddy Waters on Mick Jagger*

Everybody ask me if I sing on this record. Even my mother asks me. Fabrice and I—I think we are big talents. We can sing as

good as any other pop star in the Top Ten.
— *Rob Pilatus, Milli Vanilli*

Artists everywhere steal mercilessly all
the time and I think this is healthy.
— *Peter Gabriel*

I don't think anybody steals anything; all
of us borrow.   — *B.B. King*

All rock 'n' roll is plagiarism. I think more
people should admit it and do it better.
— *Gerard Van Herk, Deja Voodoo*

When you write a song that sounds really
good . . . you think, surely it must be
someone else's.
— *Pete Shelley, The Buzzcocks*

I sat down one night and wrote the line
rock, rock, rock everybody. I was going to
use the word "stomp"—like rock, rock,
rock and then stomp, stomp, stomp. But

that didn't fit. I went from one word to another and finally came up with "roll." It fit, because it was r and r, you know, two rs. So the lyric went rock, rock, rock everybody, roll, roll, roll everybody. So I finished the tune. . . . I asked Alan Freed to plug the record and as the record was playing over the air, he would pound the desk. He would open the tune, pounding the desk and yelling over the record—rock everybody, roll everybody, rock and roll. Alan should be given credit for the name, but it came from a song that I wrote. That's the way it was.   — *Bill Haley*

I remember the guys in the Air Force saying "Don't step on my blue suede shoes." I thought it was a good line and told Carl [Perkins] he should put it into a song. But he wrote it all. It's his song.

                                          — *Johnny Cash*

We have about four million changes in

every song—and almost every song is over five minutes long.   — *Geddy Lee, Rush*

I wouldn't go out. . . . I was scared, scared of the water. It really scared me.
                    — *Brian Wilson*

Sometimes I'm not sure what a lot of our songs are about.   — *Jim Kerr, Simple Minds*

There are moods I'm in when I can't stand to listen to some of my own music.
                    — *Joni Mitchell*

I was always wondering if they really liked me or did they like my songs?
                    — *Neil Young*

Basically we put our songs together in very much the same way the ways in Metallica do.
          — *John Flansburgh, They Might Be Giants*

I used to pretend that Tchaikovsky could compose through me, and it worked.
— *Chris Lowe, Pet Shop Boys*

I know some lines are bad when I write them. That's sort of perverted, isn't it?
— *Jane Siberry*

I refuse to slap some stupid words on the stupid paper just so we have a stupid song finished.
— *Suzanne Vega*

I knew, I had no qualms, nothing. I was going to sing, and I was going to sing rock 'n' roll.
— *Ronnie Spector*

People at school told me I couldn't make it, that I would end up making potholders.
— *Stevie Wonder*

When we were in high school, we were the only people that even played music, I mean rock.   — *Tom Fogerty*

I used to take accordion lessons. I whipped out some heavy polkas and Beatles tunes n' shit.   — *Tommy Lee, Motley Crue*

I was doing folk rock when there was no such thing as folk rock.

                    — *Roger McGuinn*

I was a punk in the Fifties.   — *Joni Mitchell*

I never had no one teach me nothing.
                    — *Willie Mae Thornton*

I don't know how—I just did it! It was just that time when anybody could form a band.   — *Poly Styrene, X-Ray Specs*

Christ was a punk rocker.   — *Billy Idol*

I have the devil in me! If I didn't I'd be a Christian!
                    — *Jerry Lee Lewis*

If you're writing songs, there are two things that you just don't write about: politics and religion. We write about both.

— *Bono*

All of the rock music being aired today is demonically inspired. Any individual listening to it is entering into communion with a wickedness and evil spawned in hell.

— *Jimmy Swaggart*

The Beatles are a passing phase. They are the symptoms of the uncertainties of the times.

— *Billy Graham*

We're more popular than Jesus Christ now. I don't know which will go first: rock 'n' roll or Christianity.

— *John Lennon*

I won't be happy until I'm as famous as God.

— *Madonna*

Bob Dylan is the closest thing to a saint that I know of among white people in America.   — *Nina Simone*

I am not a saint. I am a noise.
   — *Joan Baez*

They think we're satanic.
   — *Kurt Cobain, Nirvana*

We've made our deals with the devil.
   — *Huey Lewis*

I am the string, and the Supreme is the musician.   — *Carlos Santana*

When I do my music, I include a lot of people but nobody's really involved except myself. Just God and me. I guess I'm like Einstein—let 'em worry about my theory after I'm dead.   — *James Brown*

Instead of Messiahs we always had big

rock 'n' roll stars. We like to see who we're worshipping.   — *Patti Smith*

We were rehearsing and . . . a friend we had known came in and said "If you change your group around and glorify Jesus, you'll go straight to the top."
                    — *Robert Sweet, Stryper*

I played the piano in church. I even taught bible school one year. Then I got into The Greatest Gospel Hits of the 70s and it was all over.   — *Axl Rose, Guns N Roses*

Probably the biggest bringdown in my life was being in a pop group and finding out just how much it was like everything it was supposed to be against. — *Mama Cass Elliott*

My Daddy is my biggest fan. He's a minister, you know.
                    — *Alice Cooper*

I had it made in the heart of Cheever

country; the big house on the Sound, a
beautiful wife, two children, the luxury
car, the whole shot. But no country club,
just a $1000-a-day drug frenzy.
                              — *John Phillips*

The reason kids like rock 'n' roll is because
their parents don't.   — *Mitch Miller*

He's the King of Rock 'n' Roll.
          — *Jerry Lee Lewis's mom on Chuck Berry*

When he was three, he said he'd be a star.
                    — *Mettie Baker, Prince's mom*

My dad taught me about music. He used
to tap dance.   — *Ray Davies, The Kinks*

He was like a real dad, you know. We used
to sit down with guitars and mess around.
               — *Julian Lennon on John Lennon*

We all come from dysfunctional families

and these days I guess that's pretty normal.
— *Carnie Wilson, Wilson Phillips*

Remember when you used to watch TV in the 60s and you'd see Perry Como in a cashmere sweater? That's what rock 'n' roll is becoming. It's your parents' music.
— *Neil Young*

No matter how loud the guitar is and how much you jump around and sweat and get angst-ridden, eventually you have to go home, be polite, and kiss your mother on the cheek. — *Jim Wilbur, Superchunk*

I'm a rebel, a brat. That's the way rock musicians are. — *Bryan Adams*

I don't listen to music. I hate all music.
— *Johnny Rotten*

I never met Johnny Rotten but I like what

he did to people.   — *Neil Young*

I enjoy getting people angry and getting underneath their skin, especially people who don't think.   — *Jello Biafra*

What do bored kids do when they don't play rock 'n' roll? They torture cats, they do burglaries.   — *Kim Thayil, Soundgarden*

That's the problem that rock 'n' roll poses—to be or not to be a rebel. That's what it says and always has said.

          — *David Bowie*

Rock 'n' roll is a bit like Las Vegas; guys dressed up in their sisters' clothes pretending to be rebellious and angry but not really angry about anything.   — *Sting*

On my gravestone, I want it to say "I told you I was sick." Achievement is for the senators and scholars. At one time I had ambitions but I had them removed by a doctor in Buffalo.   — *Tom Waits*

I had to cater to guys a lot. I had to placate them, stroke them a little, and always keep my place.   — *Nancy Sinatra*

Someone said "Wear this," and we'd go "Oh, okay." The Runaways were out there just for the boys.   — *Lita Ford*

What pisses me off is when I've got seven or eight record company fat pig men sitting there telling me what to wear.
                    — *Sinead O'Connor*

Even though I was a big seller, they only cared about males.   — *Lesley Gore*

You have to be twice as smart, twice as tough, and twice as good as the men just to get to the bottom of the rank where you

can eat and pay your rent.
— *Carol Colman, Kid Creole and the Coconuts*

A lot of chicks come up to me and ask me, in fact it used to piss me off I must say, they'd say, "How does it feel being a chick playing guitar?" The minute that I would hear that remark, I would just want to hit them.
— *Alice Stuart*

After we sold three or four million albums, we thought we wouldn't be treated like an all-girl band anymore, but as a rock 'n' roll band. That never really worked.
— *Belinda Carlisle*

Rock 'n' roll is for men. Real rock 'n' roll is a man's job. I want to see a man up there. I want to see a man's muscles, a man's veins. I don't want to see no chick's tit banging against a bass.
— *Patti Smith*

What's the difference between females

playing and males playing? That we don't have dicks? — *Lori Barbero, Babes in Toyland*

The only people who can express anything new in rock are girls and gays.
— *Deborah Harry*

There are no more political statements. The only thing rock fans have in common is their music.
— *Bob Pittman, Vice-President, MTV*

Rock 'n' roll since its inception has always been more sexually subversive than politically subversive.
— *Stephen Mallinder, Cabaret Voltaire*

Pop music is usually so pretentious when it tries to be political. — *Paul Simon*

The MC5 is totally committed to the revolution. With our music and our economic genius we plunder the unsuspecting straight world for money and the means to carry out our program, and revolutionize its children at the same time.

— *John Sinclair, manager, MC5*

They worry "What are these blacks going to do after they listen to Ice Cube's record?" But ain't nothing coming off physical. It's a mental revolution we've got to go through.

— *Ice Cube*

Rap is teaching white kids what it means to be black, and that causes a problem for the infrastructure.

— *Chuck D, Public Enemy*

It's like the early days of rock 'n' roll. The authorities paid no attention as long as it was a black thing but as soon as white kids began aping black styles, they came down hard.

— *Luther Campbell, 2 Live Crew*

We started Oi . . . it was our movement,

but it was taken off us and it started to get out of hand, like a monster out of control. People think we're fascists or Nazis or nasty people, but we've all got great big hearts.
— *Mickey Geggus, The Cockney Rejects*

Who wants politics in music? I find politics the single most uninspiring, unemotional, insensitive activity on this planet.
— *Adam Ant*

I'm all for sociological lyrics. I just can't be bothered to write them.
— *Suggs, Madness*

When you're as rich as I am, you don't have to be political.
— *Sting*

Music can't change the world.
— *Bob Geldof*

Politics is a part of life, and you would be

ignoring a whole aspect of life by leaving it
out of songs.   — *Bruce Cockburn*

You can't be a politician with a guitar.
                       — *John Doe, X*

We want to be the band to dance to when
the bomb drops.
                       — *Simon LeBon, Duran Duran*

I don't even know what politics are, to tell
you the truth.   — *Bob Dylan*

I don't pretend to give a message of any
kind, except enjoy yourself and get laid.
                       — *Lemmy, Motorhead*

Rock 'n' roll meant fucking, originally—
which I don't think is a bad idea. Let's
bring it back again.   — *Waylon Jennings*

I go to the beach to get a tan. It makes my
tight little body all brown and nice, so

when we play concerts all the boys in the
audience will get a hard-on.
— *Paula Pierce, The Pandoras*

I'm still that sort to let them wet their
knickers on the seats. That's basically what
it's all about for me.   — *Cliff Richard*

The singer gets the pussy.
— *George Clinton*

My dick made the decision for me to get
into music so I could finally get fucked at
the age of 14.   — *Al Jourgensen, Ministry*

If chicks are gonna stand there and go
"Huh?" and look at each other, then I'm
wasting my time.   — *Jeff Beck*

The guys are there to make the broads, the
broads are just sittin' there waitin' for the
guys, and I'm up there on the bandstand
makin' my guitar.   — *Link Wray*

We want to be phalluses ramming in the butthole of pop.
— *Gibby Haines, Butthole Surfers*

Rock 'n' roll is trying to convince girls to pay money to be near you.
— *Richard Hell*

There's an abundance of women. Everybody wants to suck your dick.   — *Slash*

I think pop music has done more for oral intercourse than anything else that ever happened, and vice versa.   — *Frank Zappa*

What you really want to know is whether I lick pussy and stuff like that. 'Course I do.
— *Sting*

You won't make much money, but you'll get more pussy than Frank Sinatry.
— *Ronnie Hawkins to Robbie Robertson*

Ultimately, I want to make everybody horny.
— *Patti Smith*

I think it's an asset to a performer to be sexually attractive.
— *Carly Simon*

I've been known to forget to unhandcuff a few girls.
— *Stiv Bators*

Don't forget, the penis is mightier than the sword.
— *Screamin' Jay Hawkins*

If there was anything I loved better than a big penis, it was a bigger penis.
— *Little Richard*

There's no message to heavy metal. It's about being rich and famous and getting laid.
— *Penelope Spheeris*

If I was a girl, I'd rather fuck a rock star

than a plumber.

— *Gene Simmons, KISS*

There'll always be some arrogant little brat who wants to make music with a guitar. Rock 'n' roll will never die.

— *Dave Edmunds*

I started playing clarinet, but the orthodontist said I was going to have a bad overbit and that I'd better quit so I found a ukulele . . . but daddy said, "The only two big ukulele guys I can think of are Ukulele Ike and Arthur Godfrey. . . . You'd better try guitar."   — *Johnny Winter*

I actually went deaf for a period of time.

— *Eric Clapton*

I can't use right-handed instruments now because I snipped the ends of my fingers off.   — *Toni Iommi, Black Sabbath*

Five guys on stage sounding like World War III.
— *Les Paul on heavy metal*

Why the fuck hasn't there been a female Jimi Hendrix, a female guitar great? Because no one ever put in the effort and stuck to it. I thought, I'm going to get up there and fucking do it myself.
— *Lita Ford*

Rock 'n' roll is simply an attitude. You don't have to play the greatest guitar.
— *Johnny Thunders*

I smash guitars because I like them.
— *Pete Townshend*

My guitar is the only thing in my life that hasn't fucked me over.
— *Dave Mustaine, Megadeth*

My fantasy [guitar] would be a cannon

that shot sperm at the audience.
— *Angus Young, AC/DC*

I consider it my patriotic duty to keep Elvis in the 90% tax bracket.
— *Colonel Tom Parker*

The whole music business in the United States is based on numbers, based on unit sales and not based on quality. It's not based on beauty, it's based on hype and it's based on cocaine. It's based on giving presents of large packages of dollars to play records on the air.   — *Frank Zappa*

All we had ever heard about record company people was that they were vampires and criminals and they killed Elvis Presley.
— *Björk*

There always was some kind of payola, but it was much smaller than what I hear goes on today. You know, twenty dinners in a week, a hooker for the night, maybe even a color TV, but that was it.

— *Ellie Greenwich*

If I could find a white man who had the Negro sound and Negro feel, I could make a billion dollars. — *Sam Phillips*

There's three of us in the band so we split everything straight down the middle.

— *Mitch Mitchell, Jimi Hendrix Experience*

All I know, this guy came to me, he wanted to make a record and he told me I'm gonna be rich. That's what I expected. I expected to be rich for making a record and it didn't materialize.

— *Lil Rodney Cee, Funky Four Plus One More*

You're a local band until you get a record contract, then all of a sudden Bruce Springsteen is your competition.

— *Sammy Llana, The Bodeans*

With the punk thing, everyone was making impractical attacks on being rich or having money, y'know, but they all wanted to be rich.

— *Boy George*

We don't get down on our knees and say, "I want to be a star. I will look it, act it, dress it, be it. Make me one." ... We'll probably end up being something really boring like fuckin' REO [Speedwagon], who were around for nine years before they made it.

— *Paul Westerberg, The Replacements*

In the 60s, rock was a scary proposition in most corporate boardrooms. It became the antithesis of materialism and the corporate American way. But in the 80s, that no longer hold true.

— *Danny Socolof, President, MEGA*

It's irrelevant whether Michael Jackson drinks Pepsi or Duran Duran drinks Coke.

What's relevant is what these groups stand for and what their sponsors hope to stand for by tying in with them.
— *Allen Rosenshine, chairman, BBDO (Pepsi's ad agency)*

I personally do not consider Pepsi-Cola or Old Style Beer or the Health and Tennis Corporation to be the enemy. This is the age of adult rock stars. You can't be James Dean all of your life. — *Glenn Frey*

Don't try to explain it; just sell it.
— *Colonel Tom Parker*

I think I'm very entertaining and I think I deserve all the money I get!
— *Gary Glitter*

I remember calling up Variety and accusing the Beatles of stealing my look. The woman there said "Look, sir, let me tell you something. Their hair is like the

Three Stooges, not yours!"   — *Tiny Tim*

The worst thing that ever happened to me was when platforms went out of style.
                    — *John Oates, Hall & Oates*

I look at what's there. What's there is legs and hair.   — *Tina Turner*

We're a very special group that deals in a lot of emotion and color and staying thin and getting up there and doing it. A band that can look this good and play this well has something to prove across America.
                    — *Michael Aston, Gene Loves Jezebel*

We like to look sixteen and bored shitless.
                    — *David Johansen, New York Dolls*

Rock 'n' roll is not so much a question of electric guitars as it is striped pants.
                    — *David Lee Roth*

People used to throw rocks at me for my clothes. Now they wanna know where I buy them.   — *Cyndi Lauper*

I taught Madonna how to fucking wear tights, man. I'm so happy someone else's doing it. Now maybe they won't look at the color of my panties, and they can concentrate on my singing.   — *Pat Benetar*

Everybody expects us to walk around with socks on our dicks.
          — *Anthony Kiedis, Red Hot Chili Peppers*

I'm not trying to sell sex. I just don't like wearing a lot of clothes onstage.
          — *Sheila E.*

I'd rather be dead than singing "Satisfaction" when I'm 45.   — *Mick Jagger*

Thirty years in the same location, we're still churning it out. If you like it, it's here and you know where to get it.

> — *Keith Richards*

We're the McDonald's of rock. We're always there to satisfy, and a billion served.

> — *Paul Stanley, KISS*

I wouldn't like in fifteen years time to still be playing "Crocodile Rock."

> — *Elton John (1975)*

It's been like a bad dream I never woke up from.

> — *Alex Chilton*

We're fucking 40-year-old men, and we're behaving like children. It's silly, absolutely fucking idiotic. Retarded.

> — *Eric Burdon*

I may be a living legend, but that sure don't help when I've got to change a flat tire.

> — *Roy Orbison*

If you're in this business for more than five years, you become a boring old fart.
— *Brian Travers, UB40*

Making a comeback is one of the most difficult things to do with dignity.
— *Greg Lake, ELP*

There won't be a Beatles reunion as long as John Lennon remains dead.
— *George Harrison*

I thought we stood for infinity.
— *Mick Jagger*

The Beatles are not merely awful; they are so unbelievably horrible, so appallingly unmusical, so dogmatically insensitive to the magic of the art, that they qualify as crowned head of anti-music.
— *William F. Buckley, Jr.*

Reeling like a top, snapping his fingers

and jerking his eyeballs, with hair like something Medusa had sent back, and a voice that was enormously improved by total unintelligibility.

— *John Crosby on Fabian (1960)*

He [Phil Spector] was gonna shoot us. He started a fight . . . a publicity stunt. He drove me to beating him up. We were prisoners in his house for about six hours, and we thought we were gonna get shot.

— *Johnny Ramone*

A lot of Michael's success is due to timing and luck. It could just as easily have been me.

— *Jermaine Jackson*

Quite simply, I feel that the Stones are the world's best rock 'n' roll band.

— *Pete Townshend*

Sometimes I really do believe that we're the only rock band on the face of this

planet that knows what rock 'n' roll is all about.
— *Pete Townshend*

Rock and roll really changed my life. I heard Little Richard and Jerry Lee Lewis and that was it.
— *Elton John*

Everybody I've seen like Little Richard, Jerry Lee Lewis, and all those sort of people, I'm afraid, are extremely pathetic.
— *Elton John*

Led Zepplin is just a bunch of stupid idiots who wrote cool riffs.
— *Chris Cornell, Soundgarden*

I could never get along in a band with a posturing, posing lead singer.
— *Keith Richards on Led Zepplin*

Mick Jagger is about as sexy as a pissing toad.
— *Truman Capote*

Groups like Genesis and Yes are about as exciting as used Kleenex. It might as well be Tony Bennett.   — *Nick Lowe*

I will sit down with anybody that has criticised my work negatively; I will sit down with them and make them eat shit.
    — *August Darnell, Kid Creole and The Coconuts*

I will personally cut off my dick and eat it! I will cut my cock off on the Ed Sullivan show and chew on it. That is what I'll do if the new album bombs.   — *Ted Nugent*

I'm actually quite a decent chap and the rest of the group are wankers.
    — *Jools Holland, Squeeze*

The Sex Pistols are like some contagious disease.   — *Malcolm McLaren*

Malcolm McLaren is the greatest conman that I ever met.   — *Johnny Thunders*

I think he's great, brilliant, but he's just
there like Harrod's or Frank Sinatra.
— *Boy George on David Bowie*

I've looked up to David Bowie all my life
but now I think he should look up to us.
— *Ian McCulloch, Echo & The Bunnymen*

If you want to torture me you'd tie me
down and force me to watch our first five
videos.   — *Jon Bon Jovi*

Comparing Madonna with Marilyn Mon-
roe is like comparing Raquel Welch with
the back of a bus.   — *Boy George*

Boy George makes me sick.   — *Madonna*

Madonna is closer to organized prostitu-
tion than anything else.   — *Morrissey*

I was considering doing a song with Billy
Idol. That would have been good because

we're both white and plastic and blonde.

— *Madonna*

White people should make rock 'n' roll . . . that's white music. They can't really make black music.   — *Billy Idol*

If I'm considered part of that overhyped, overproduced, overindulgent supergroup style, then I'm bummed.

— *Billy Joel*

Steve can go off and be Peter Frampton; Sid can go off and kill himself and nobody will care; Paul can go back to being an electrician; and Malcolm will always be a Wally.   — *Johnny Rotten on the disintegration of the Sex Pistols*

I can't do anything else.   — *Jerry Garcia*

You have official Urge permission to

make up our quotes.
— *Blackie Onassis, Urge Overkill*

Nobody can do it as good as me.
— *Joey Shithead, DOA*

Let's face it, I'm a showoff.
— *Peter Frampton*

I believe my music is the healin' music. I believe my music can make the blind see, the lame walk, the deaf and dumb hear and talk, because it inspires and uplifts people. It regenerates the heart, makes the liver quiver, the bladder splatter and the knees freeze. I'm not conceited either.
— *Little Richard*

I am the Nureyev of rock 'n' roll.
— *Meat Loaf*

I'm an instant star: just add water and stir.
— *David Bowie*

I thank you in advance for the great round of applause I am about to get. — *Bo Diddley*

My ego is already inflated way past the exploding stage.   — *Kurt Cobain, Nirvana*

I am bringing my genius to idiots who cannot go out and reach it for themselves because they are too stupid.

— *The Great Kat*

I'm ambitious. But if I weren't as talented as I am ambitious, I would be a gross monstrousity.   — *Madonna*

They call me "the Godfather of Soul." None of the new generation can ever be Godfather. The only people that qualify are myself and Sinatra.   — *James Brown*

It's actually come as quite a shock to learn just how many people don't like me.

— *Phil Collins*

The biggest misconception people have about me is that I'm stupid. — *Billy Idol*

I'm always trying to figure out why people don't appreciate Duran Duran.
— *John Taylor, Duran Duran*

In Japan, they named a Sake after me.
— *Suzi Quatro*

People lead really flat lives. They need a sort of peak. I like to be that peak.
— *Michael Hutchence, INXS*

The whole business is built on ego, vanity, self-satisfaction and it's total crap to pretend it's not. — *George Michael*

The business we are in is the advertising business, and that's the only business any radio station should be in.
— *Dave Shepperd, KRES, Moberly, Missouri*

Alan Freed jumped into radio like a stripper into Swan Lake. He was a teenager's mind funneled into 50,000 watts.

— *Clark Whelton*, New York Times

In the Top 40, half the songs are *secret* messages to the teen world to drop out, turn on, and groove with the chemicals and light shows at discotheques.

— *Art Linkletter*

In the States, if you put out something that sounds like it was recorded in a toilet, which is what rock 'n' roll is essentially, you can't get it on the radio. The Top 100 is the same old schlock they've been peddling for ten years.

— *John Hiatt*

I haven't been sent a turd, but some chap in Manchester who took exception to The Damned wiped his bum and sent me the piece of paper through the mail which wasn't too charming.

— *John Peel, BBC*

Tell the world we're synthetic because, damn it, we are. The music had nothing to do with us. It was totally dishonest.

— *Mike Nesmith, The Monkees*

I've gone through a whoring stage. That's fine, it's good to learn what it's like to be a whore.

— *Perry Farrell, Jane's Addiction*

I'm not riding on the Beatles' coattails. If they go, I'm going to be ready for the next person that comes along.

— *Murray the K*

The only thing that keeps half the people alive in factories is the fucking radio on all day.

— *Johnny Rotten*

The Mersey Sound is the voice of 80,000 crumbling houses and 30,000 people on the dole.

— *The Daily Worker (1963)*

We punched a clock, literally punched a clock nine o'clock in the morning. That was the procedure at Motown. Berry Gordy had worked at Ford, so he ran Motown like a factory.

— *Lamont Dozier*

That was one of the unique things about Motown. There were no set hours to do anything. — *Levi Stubbs*

A musician should be as much a part of a community as a bricklayer or a shop-keeper. — *Stuart Adamson, Big Country*

A recording studio is not much different from a factory. It's just a factory for music.

— *Van Morrison*

I think of what we do as the equivalent of working at Lockheed. Writing songs is being in research and development. making records is production and going out on tour is sales. We're going out to sell our B-1 bomber.

— *David Weiss, Was (Not Was)*

Being spokesman for a generation is the worst job I ever had.

— *Billy Bragg*

If anything, rock 'n' roll should fit the proletarian view of art, which is partly what made punk so powerful.

— *Jerry Harrison*

The way I see it, rock 'n' roll is folk music.

— *Robert Plant*

If I told you what our music is really about, we'd probably all get arrested.

— *Bob Dylan*

Since every record released surely contains something offensive to someone, sticker them all. Make this as meaningless as the bar code.
                                        — *Michael Stipe*

I don't want my album coming out with a G rating. Nobody would buy it.
— *Donny Osmond on the Parents' Music Resource Center*

You're talking to someone to really understands rock music.
                                — *Tipper Gore, PMRC*

There is always gonna be an element that doesn't like rock 'n' roll. But as long as I keep it clean and within FCC guidelines, I say "Fuck 'em."
— *Charlie Kendall, WNEW-FM, New York on the PMRC*

When it comes to the minds and hairdos of our young people, something had to be

done.
— *George Bush on the CIA investigation of the highly suspect number of British rock bands signed to American recording contracts*

I can't say "fuck" on a record. Fuck is a nice word. Fuck means something pretty. I like fuck. And I can't say it on a record.
— *David Crosby*

Where do you go from Elvis Presley—short of obscenity, which is against the law?
— *John Crosby,*
New York Herald Tribune *(1956)*

Music has helped society accept gay sexuality because of the weird creatures on TV—Boy George, Marilyn, Freddie Mercury.
— *Paul Rutherford, Frankie Goes to Hollywood*

You now have a nation of kids who don't read. The bulk of information that enters

their brains comes from television or records . . . so control over those sources of
information is rather attractive to an au-
thoritarian mentality.

— *Frank Zappa*

It's got a good beat. You can dance to it. I
like the words. I'll give it a 98.
— *Bobby, 14, American Bandstand (1958)*

I don't set trends. I just find out what they
are and exploit them.   — *Dick Clark*

It ain't easy to get it so I'm not hand
twirling when the others are doing some
hip thing!   — *Barbara Lee, The Chiffons*

I practice at home. I try to invent moves,
and when I get something I like I videotape
it.   — *David Byrne*

You could live in Winnipeg a thousand
years and not meet Ringo, Paul

McCartney and Bob Dylan.
— *Burton Cummings*

I've got a phone, answer machine, TV set, computer, hand grenade—everything you need to run a business in Los Angeles.
— *Ice-T*

I'd like to say that we're not boring. We play great music and we're exciting. We jump about and wiggle our bums.
— *Joe Strummer, The Clash*

I'm leaving the group. I want a divorce.
— *John Lennon*

I'd rather have ten years of super-hypermost than live to be seventy by sitting in some goddamn chair watching TV.
— *Janis Joplin*

I'm the one that's got to die when it's time for me to die, so let me live my life the way

I want to.
                              — *Jimi Hendrix*

Nobody deserves to have their personal life pried into like I did and no one deserves to hear me whine about it so much.
                              — *Kurt Cobain, Nirvana*

I like to think of us as Clearasil on the face of the nation. Jim Morrison would have said that if he was smart, but he's dead.
                              — *Lou Reed*

I certainly thought of going to see Sid Vicious and trying to say something to him that would cool him out and make it all okay.
                              — *Paul McCartney*

There is nothing about my career that is an accident.
                              — *Marc Bolan*

I went into the closet and said "I'm gonna kill myself." There was chlorine bleach and I said "Nah, that's gonna taste bad." So

I took the Pledge. And all I ended up doing was farting furniture polish. — *Billy Joel*

Just rock on, and have you a good time.
— *Duane Allman*

I never thought I was wasted, but I probably was. — *Keith Richards*

The truth is where the truth is and sometimes it's in the candy store. — *Bob Dylan*

Marijuana took rock 'n' roll into the future, and rock 'n' roll took marijuana to the masses so they could climb into the future too, and nobody's ever been the same since. — *John Sinclair*

Everybody gets fucked up, man. Everybody gets fucked up sooner or later. You're just pretending if you don't let your music get just as liquid as you are when you're high. — *Neil Young*

I drink beer. I smoke some pot. I don't think I have a drug problem.
— *Flea, Red Hot Chili Peppers*

I used to rhyme for hours. Drink a 40-ounce beer, Olde English, and I wouldn't be able to shut up for the whole day and the whole night.
— *Daryll McDaniels, Run-DMC*

We couldn't do the amount of drugs we wanted and be a band, so we ended up doing the drugs.
— *Paul McKenzie, Enigmas*

I didn't really want to enjoy the moment. I wanted to take drugs.
— *Doug Fleger, The Knack*

I was a successful junkie for about a year; the only reason I was able to stay healthy and didn't have to rob houses was because

I had a lot of money.

— *Kurt Cobain, Nirvana*

While I was a junkie I learned to ski and made *Exile On Main St.*   — *Keith Richards*

I was basically on about a triple acid trip right when they asked me to play at Woodstock. Which answers the question: Can a man play his own songs when he couldn't find his car?   — *John Sebastian*

I definitely have a responsibility to talk negatively about heroin. It's a really really evil drug—I think opiates are directly linked to Satan.   — *Kurt Cobain, Nirvana*

Take the drugs away and there's more time for sex and rock 'n' roll.
— *Steven Tyler, Aerosmith, after 4 rehab sessions*

The fun thing about being sober is meeting all the friends I've had for years—especially the ones I've never met.

— *Alice Cooper*

I've led a pretty clean life so I've aged pretty well.   — *Bobby Sherman*

Like when you wake up that morning and as soon as you're awake enough to remember, "Oh, I'm goin' to a concert tonight," you call up your best friend. You get excited, you figure out what you're wearing, you decide where you're gonna meet, and then you meet and you go to the venue, and you see all these other people, and you get more excited. Then the opening act comes on, and you're more excited. And the lights go down and: whoa!   — *Joan Jett*

For me it was like I was an old car and I was being taken out for a ride at 100 miles an hour, and I kind of like it because I was

really getting rid of a lot of rust.
— *Norman Mailer on a Ramones concert*

I wanted to get up and dance but I wasn't allowed to in the Royal Box.
— *Princess Diana on Dire Straits concert*

Onstage I've been hit by a grapefruit, beercans, eggs, spit, money, cigarette butts, Mandies, Quaaludes, joints, bras, panties and a fist.
— *Iggy Pop*

I like leaping around on stage as long as it's done with class.
— *Richie Blackmore, Deep Purple*

Nobody could ever hear us anyway. There was always too much noise.
— *Mark Lindsay, Paul Revere and The Raiders*

We became professional room-clearers.
— *Jean Smith, Mecca Normal*

A rock 'n' roll band needs to be able to get under people's skin. You should be able to clear the room at the drop of a hat.
— *Paul Westerberg, The Replacements*

On stage I make love to 25,000 people, then I go home alone. — *Janis Joplin*

Inside the clubs it's alright; outside we get the shit kicked out of us.
— *Perry Farrell, Jane's Addiction*

If you're talking right at the kids you're singing to, then the audience feels it too. That's our soul. It's got nothing to do with colour. When you see the audiences grooving, and you know everything just clicks, that's soul. — *Betty, The Shangri-Las*

Nothin disappoints me more than when I see someone who's lost in the groove and feelin' good and then a Doc Marten smacks 'em in the bridge of the nose.

Don't get me wrong, I'm not preaching against moshing and stage-diving. Because I provoke it a lot and I love to see people have a good time.

— *Shannon Hoon, Blind Melon*

We go home safe in the knowledge that we've deafened a few.

— *Phil Taylor, Motorhead*

It's the most over-milked, watered-down bullshit I've ever seen, this damn encore stuff.

— *Black Francis, The Pixies*

There is no live set. I just make it up as I go along.

— *Jonathan Richman*

In the Asian concerts and the military shows they want the old stuff, which is really a bummer for us.

— *Don Wilson, The Ventures*

Some of the things I used to see from the

stage! You'd probably think it was nothing, but this woman, one of the stripteasers, would take her drawers off and men would come up to her and they'd start doing—Aw, man! She was too funky! That, to me, was awful. — *Michael Jackson*

All my concerts had no sounds in them: they were completely silent. People had to make their own music in their minds.

— *Yoko Ono*

If we stay in small clubs, we'll develop small minds, and then we'll develop small music. — *Bono, U2*

We didn't even know we were the Beach Boys until the song came out.

— *Mike Love*

Taxi drivers, our mothers, feminists, men—no one liked it. It was obscene to

everybody.   — *Viv Albertine on the name*
of her band, The Slits

I wake up some nights and think Orchestral Manoeuvres In The Dark? What a stupid name! Why did we pick that one?
    — *Andy McCluskey, OMD*

You can call me Jimmy or you can call me Iggy. My parents called me James Osterberg Jr. Iggy was a nickname hung on me that I didn't particularly like.
    — *Iggy Pop*

I always like sort of funny, corny, pompous stage names, like Iggy Pop and Billy Idol. My father suggested Black Francis; it's an old family name.
    — *Black Francis, The Pixies*

This big rat just happened to scuttle along at the very moment I was telling them I had scabies.   — *Rat Scabies*

If anybody asks you what kind of music you play, tell him "pop." Don't tell him "rock 'n' roll" or they won't even let you in the hotel.   — *Buddy Holly*

Just because you call yourself psychedelic doesn't mean you are psychedelic.
                    — *Richard Butler, Psychedelic Furs*

We always hated being called an art band. I never took art in high school.
                    — *Thurston Moore, Sonic Youth*

We're labelling it "soul bubblegum."
                    — *Berry Gordy on the Jackson 5*

We'd never heard of the movie. It just sounded like a funny name. Then I found out about the film and saw it. I hated it.
                    — *Kevin Shields, My Bloody Valentine*

Grunge is a really neat word. It was a good

marketing term, it has a nice ring to it.
— *Dave Crider, Mono Men*

I don't know what grunge is. That's like buildup on your windows.
— *Jerry Cantrell, Alice in Chains*

I'm very driven even though I don't drive.
— *Debbie Gibson*

I always start out the first week I'm on tour running every day. I try to eat right. Then there's always a night when I didn't get enough sleep so I don't run, and I'm afraid of eating so I do some cocaine, and I was depressed that night so I take an upper, and then that's the end of it. Then it's uppers and coke for the rest of the tour.
— *Linda Ronstadt*

Being on tour sends me crazy. I drink too much and out comes the John McEnroe in me.
— *Chrissie Hynde, The Pretenders*

I would think nothing of tipping over a table with a whole long spread on it just because there was turkey roll on the table and I had explicitly said "No turkey roll."

— *Steven Tyler, Aerosmith*

We were barred from so many hotels— the entire Holiday Inn chain—that we had to check in as Fleetwood Mac lots of times.

— *Ronnie Wood on the Faces*

There isn't a town in the world I haven't run amok in.   — *Joe Strummer, The Clash*

You look for certain things in certain towns. Chicago, for example, is notorious for sort of two things at once—balling two chicks, or three—in combination acts.

— *Jimmy Page, Led Zeppelin*

Nowadays we're more into staying in our rooms and reading Nietzsche.

— *Jimmy Page*

There aren't as many groupies as there used to be.

— *K.K. Downing, Judas Priest*

I wouldn't say we have a publicity strategy for this tour. The Stones, we believe, make their own news.

— *David Horowitz, publicist for the Stones' American tour, 1969*

Most of these young bands did not have to break the paths D.O.A. or Black Flag did, where you would play and go to the club owner, say, "Can we have our money?" and he would hold a billy club and say, "Let's fight for it."

— *Henry Rollins*

Being on the road hasn't tarnished our viewpoints toward women. If anything, it's made us better in bed.

— *Dave Mustaine, Megadeth*

I imagine there's all kinds of screams that guys are doin' are off-key. Like James, he'll scream between the notes. He screams, but nobody never knows what key he's in! But I scream on key.

— *Wilson Pickett*

The better the singer's voice, the harder it is to believe what they're saying, so I used my faults to an advantage.   — *David Byrne*

A singer really was the last thing I wanted to be.   — *David Bowie*

I'm not really a good singer. But most people aren't either.   — *Robyn Hitchcock*

Anybody that walks can sing.

— *Michael Stipe, R.E.M.*

I can hardly sing, you know what I mean? I'm no Tom Jones and I couldn't give a fuck.   — *Mick Jagger*

Everybody gives off a certain musical note. I think I'm F-sharp. The thing is is you can go around and you meet somebody who's in F-sharp, you're in harmony, see. But if you meet somebody who's in F—unng—it's a discord: you don't get on.
— *Donovan*

We just did our own thing which was a combination of rock 'n' roll, and Fellini, and game-show host, and corn, and mysticism.
— *Fred Schneider, The B-52s*

Ringo played the backbeat and never got off it. Man, you couldn't have moved him with a crane.
— *D.J. Fontana*

I like Beethoven, especially the poems.
— *Ringo Starr*

The best bit is just knowing you can stay in bed if you want to.
— *Roland Gift, Fine Young Cannibals*

I'm barely prolific and incredibly lazy.
— *Tom Petty*

The white youth of today have begun to react to the fact that the "American Way of Life" is a fossil of history. . . . All they know is that it feels good to swing to way-out body-rhythms instead of dragassing across the dance floor like zombies to the dead beat of mind-smothering Mickey Mouse music.   — *Eldridge Cleaver*

Our main audience is about 18 years old. People that age don't really understand music that much. . . . If they were really that musically hip, they wouldn't even like us.   — *Richie Blackmore, Deep Purple*

The typical rock fan isn't smart enough to know when he's being dumped on.
— *Frank Zappa*

I think we have good taste and a good

audience. They aren't too much into herpes.   — *Rudolf Schenker, Scorpions*

The only reason we wore sunglasses onstage was because we couldn't stand the sight of the audience.   — *John Cale*

The life of a rock 'n' roll band will last as long as you look down into the audience and can see yourself, and your audience looks up at you and can see themselves.
                      — *Bruce Springsteen*

What people say means absolutely nothing. When the record comes out it's like a receipt for me to say "fuck off."
                      — *Bill Laswell, Material*

I live pretty much of a normal life and do all the things other kids do. I don't know why everyone thinks I'm so much different.
                      — *Michael Jackson*

I happen to think they're into me, they have a certain amount of intelligence.

— *Billy Joel*

Girl-type screams are silly. When you get a guy that screams, an appreciative-type yell, encouragement, that can kind of turn you on when you're performing.

— *Rod Stewart*

I think heavy metal fans are more open-minded than people give them credit for.

— *Bruce Dickinson, Iron Maiden*

That's what we're all about; taking advantage of people.   — *Lars Ulrich, Metallica*

We had the whole nine yards. The hair-pulling, gouging, ripping the clothes and running for your life.

— *Bobby Hatfield, Righteous Brothers*

People should realize, we are just jerks like

them.   — *Bono, U2*

The people who still listen to my music
understand that I never meant them any
harm.   — *Captain Beefheart*

Just because you like my stuff doesn't
mean I owe you anything.   — *Bob Dylan*

I wish I could tell our audience that we
don't hate them without sounding cheesy.
                              — *Kurt Cobain, Nirvana*

Rock 'n' roll music is here to stay.
                              — *Alan Freed (1956)*

Index

DIVINE LABORATORIES is a Vancouver-based collective made up of musicians and those involved in the business of music.

It is the purpose of Little Red Books to gather the essential wisdom of great women and men into single volumes so that students of the Great might judge them in light of their own words, and find where they will the spiritual, sporting, political, musical and gardening models so earnestly sought after by the young, and so easily forgotten by the old.

LITTLE RED BOOKS

The Little Black & White Book of Film Noir

The Little Blonde Book of Kim Campbell

The Little Blue Book of UFOs

The Little Book of Reform

The Little Book of Wrinkles

The Little Green Book

The Little Greenish-Brown Book of Slugs

The Little Grey Flannel Book

The Little Lavender Book

The Little Pink Pink

Quotations for a Nation

Quotations from Chairman Ballard

Quotations from Chairman Cherry

Quotations from Chairman Lamport

Quotations from Chairman Zalm

Quotations on the Great One